Blue Jean Wisdom For Teens (And Others)

By

Tim A. Gaertner
With Jenna Urban
Marissa Markey
And Annie Grauf

ISBN. 978-0-9777381-2-0

Introduction

This book is a simple look at words
of wisdom.
The opinions included are NOT the only
meanings for each saying.
Some of your thoughts on each piece
of wisdom might be different than ours.
That's OK.
I left the opposite page empty for to write
what you think each saying or proverb
means to you.
Discussing each one with someone else may
bring out even more different meanings.

THANKS

I am grateful to the following people for helping me with this book.

EMILY MORRIS
JAN and JENNA URBAN
ANN NEUMEIER
TOM JAREMA
LOIS FIELD
JOHN BUSHROE
JENNI FULLER
TAYLOR THOMPSON
PAT THOMPSON
BILL O' BRIEN
WENDY MORRISSEY
And
SEAN SEAL

Dedicated

to

Ivan J. Roggen M.D.

and

Timothy A. Smith M.D.

For their help with my asthma.

And my wife Karen
for all her support.

Your Thoughts

Wisdom Is Only Found In Truth

Goethe

There is a nugget of wisdom buried within
all proverbs.
You may not agree with it at the time,
but some truth is there. Keep an open mind
while reading them.

*Jenna: This is a simple lesson. You can
learn something from everything and
everyone.*

*Marissa: Lies will only dig you a very deep
hole. The truth will make you a very wise
person and will gain you a lot of respect.*

*Annie: Awareness of the truth leads to
wisdom and growth. Lies lead to
heartbreak and more deception.*

Your Thoughts

No One Is Better Than You And You Are No Better Than Anyone Else

Unknown

This is a simple saying to keep everything
in perspective.
If you were raised in a dysfunctional family your
self-esteem may be low, making you feel everyone
is better than you.
This is simply NOT true.
For those with low self-esteem it will help to repeat
this saying every day.

Annie: Everyone was created equal, but everyone is special in their own way.

Marissa: I give you a challenge—when you wake up every morning, look into the mirror and repeat this quote.

Jenna: In high school it seems many people are judged to be better than others because of wealth or their possessions. In life these things do not matter, it is who you are inside and how you act towards others.

Your Thoughts

It Takes Two To Make A Quarrel But Only One To End It

Nicaraguan Proverb

You always have a choice with any argument.
You have choice to walk away.
A choice to see continuing the argument doesn't
make any sense. You have a choice to wait until
your emotions quiet down. You have choice to
realize you may not be totally right. You have a
choice to look at the problem from both sides.

*Jenna: This really relates to me and my
parents. Sometimes I'm too stubborn to
even listen to them.*

*Annie: You can be the bigger person,
choose the high road and take another
look at how would be the best way to
handle the situation.*

*Marissa: Don't be afraid to stand up for
yourself. If someone has wronged you, let
them know in a kind but firm way. If you
have hurt someone, apologize!*

Your Thoughts

Learn How To Say "NO"

Unknown

Learning how to say "No" is a life skill everyone needs to learn.
Have you ever said "Yes" to a friend's request all the while burning inside and wishing you had the guts to say "No"?
Just learn to say "No".
You don't need to apologize or explain why you can't do something.

Annie: Take a deep breath before deciding between saying "yes" or "no".

Jenna: Sometimes I feel taken advantage of because I am afraid to say "no", and am too worried about making someone mad. I think it is important that I learn to say "no" to stop those feelings.

Marissa: If you won't do something on your own to impress yourself, you shouldn't do it for someone else to impress them.

Your Thoughts

Right, Wrong, Or Indifferent You Are Entitled To Your Feelings

Unknown

They are your feelings.
With time, your feelings may change.
Within reason, let your feelings come out.
If it is anger, with a bit of caution, let it come out.
One word of caution may be necessary.
In dangerously dysfunctional families expressing
your feelings may have to be tempered.
Find a trusted adult outside your family to express
your feelings if it is dangerous.

Jenna: You need to be open with your feelings. Don't be afraid to speak up.

Marissa: Don't follow someone else's ideas. You ARE entitled to your own feelings.

Annie: You have a right to feel how you want to. We are each unique individuals. But always remember, when you feel bad there are ways to make yourself feel better.

Your Thoughts

Always Give Your Enemies A Way To Retreat And Save Face

Sun-tzu (The Art Of War)

An enemy cornered will fight viciously because
they have no options left. An enemy who
loses face will be extremely difficult to deal with.
A bit of compassion from you so your enemy isn't
humiliated could provide
benefits later. Learn to treat your enemy
with respect.

*Annie: We are all faced at times in our
lives when we realize we've made
a mistake. Allow others to
back down gracefully.*

*Marissa: Don't drag on a situation
longer than necessary. It is best to agree
to disagree and move on.*

*Jenna: Everyone deserves a second
chance. Don't force someone into an
uncomfortable position when they may
have made a mistake and are willing to
apologize and make things better.*

Your Thoughts

Whatever You Are Trying To Avoid Won't Go Away Until You Confront It

Anon.

You can run from your problems but you can't hide.
At some point, perhaps with professional help,
it may be best to face any problem and resolve it.
You are much stronger than you realize.

Marissa: Face your issues head on. The more you run away from the situation, the bigger it is going to get.

Annie: Pretending a problem doesn't exist often allows time for the problem to grow and get worse. No matter how much time has gone by, it needs to be taken care of.

Jenna: The longer you try to run from a problem, the worse it will get. Don't be afraid to confront it.

Your Thoughts

All The World's A Stage And All The Men And Women, Merely Players; They Have Their Exits And Their Entrances, And One Man In His Time Plays Many Parts

Shakespeare

At times we are all fools, heroes, sages, and always human.

Jenna: People change a lot, especially in high school. High school is a time when people mature and become smarter. Never hold a grudge from the past because more than likely that person will have changed over the years.

Marissa: People enter and exit your life for many reasons. Some may stay while others are gone forever, but they all have a significant affect on you and who you will become.

Annie: In life there is a beginning and an end——in between we play many parts.

Your Thoughts

He Who Holds The Stirrup Is As Good As He Who Mounts The Horse

Scottish Proverb

How often have you thought yourself superior to people who work behind the counter of a fast food restaurant? You are no better than them and they aren't any better than you. What would happen if no one did the jobs YOU feel are beneath you? Not much would get done, would it?

Jenna: We are all equal no matter what position we hold in life.

Annie: Each person plays a very important role in life. What would happen if no one ever wanted to do the things you see as less dignified or less important?

Marissa: Team work is very important in any aspect of life. Be a team player and know your role. You may not always need to be the "quarterback" or the star. If you support and give your all, people will want to be on your team.

Your Thoughts

We Must Accept
What We Cannot Change

Spanish Proverb

Much of what happens in your life you will
be powerless to change.
You can get mad at yourself, others, or even GOD but
the situation isn't going to change.
Why waste energy on something you can't do
anything about?
With acceptance you may become open to options you
didn't see before.

*Annie: Make the best out of what has been
given to you.*

*Marissa: Love your situation in life to the
best of your ability while you have it.
Whatever "it " is could be gone when you
wake up in the morning.*

*Jenna: One of my coaches told me that
you have to look at your mistake, realize
what you did wrong and move on. You
can't change the past, but you can stop
yourself from making the same mistakes
in the future.*

Your Thoughts

Only Two Things Are Infinite, The Universe And Human Stupidity, And I'm Not Sure About The Universe

Albert Einstein

When you think you have seen the most stupid action anyone could ever do, there is always a level below that.

Marissa: If you think BEFORE you act, you will never fall into this category.

Jenna: This quote makes me laugh. It eases the pain of an embarrassing moment and reassures me that somewhere, someone has done something worse than I have and they are still okay.

Annie: There is no end to the stupid things that humans do.

Your Thoughts

Those Who Talk Don't Know, Those Who Know Don't Talk

Taoist Wisdom

Have you ever met someone who tried to convince
you to believe something which wasn't true?
You knew right away they didn't know what they
were talking about.
Those who know don't always feel the
need to speak.

*Annie: "Talk is cheap". Just because
someone can say what you want to hear
doesn't mean they know their subject.*

*Marissa: The reason this rings so true is
because the person who isn't blabbing is
listening and ready to learn more from
the people around them.*

*Jenna: Some people will talk to sound
smart, possibly trying to convince
themselves they know what they're talking
about. But if you ask any questions they
may not know the answers.*

Your Thoughts

If You Make Yourself A Doormat, People Will Wipe Their Feet On You

Belizean Proverb

If you feel people treat you like a doormat it may
mean your self-esteem is low.
This low opinion of yourself CAN be improved.
It may take professional help to change those
negative feelings and be able to see you really are
a valuable person.
It may take courage to ask for help.
YOU CAN DO IT.

Annie: If you allow people to take
advantage of you they will see this as a
weakness. They will continue to use you to
get what they desire.

Jenna: In high school I always thought
people took advantage of me, but I
continued letting them. It took a long
time for me to be able to say "NO" instead
of agreeing to do anything I was
asked to do.

Marissa: The exact moment you feel you
are being used, stop it! Don't make
excuses or tell yourself "just after I do this
one more thing". You will never stop if
you are already making excuses.
Don't let anyone walk on you!

Your Thoughts

Kindness In Words Creates Confidence.
Kindness In Thinking Creates Profoundness.
Kindness In Giving Creates Love

Lao-tzu

Doing simple acts of kindness without expecting something in return will change you.
When no longer focused only on yourself you become powerful, causing much good in the world.

Jenna: It doesn't matter how you show kindness, but that you are putting others before yourself.

Marissa: Random acts of kindness should never be put on display. Don't do things for material reward or public recognition.

Annie: Kind thoughts can lead to knowing yourself and others better. Kind thoughts create bonds of love. Live as you wish to be remembered—whether it is providing kindness through thoughts, words, or deeds.

Your Thoughts

Wherever You Go, You Can't Get Rid Of Yourself

Polish Proverb

The one person you can't run from is yourself.
It could be family problems which are causing you
to feel so mixed up.
Professional help may be needed to help you
understand your feelings.
For ALL your problems there is help available.
Some agencies are based on an ability to pay so
lack of money should not be an excuse.
You DO have the courage to ask for help.

Jenna: How often do people find themselves torn up inside over a problem which could be helped by other people?

Annie: Live your life so you can be proud of who you are. You will have to live with yourself the rest of your life.

Marissa: There is a commercial that states "love the skin you're in". Know and love every little quirk you have. After all, you are all you've got.

Your Thoughts

When I Do Good, I Feel Good.
When I Do Bad, I Feel Bad.
And That Is My Religion

Abraham Lincoln

Your happiness or sadness often comes down to
such simple choices as doing good or doing bad.
Do good things with your life.

*Marissa: Think of it this way: instead of
looking for a role model, be the role
model people are looking for.*

*Jenna: You know when you've done the
wrong thing because you have a guilty
conscience. It works the same when you
do something good, you feel good.*

*Annie: Practice what makes you and
those around you feel good.*

Your Thoughts

It Is Comparison That Makes Men Happy Or Miserable

Anon.

Once you begin comparing yourself or what you
have to others there may be no end to your misery.
The person you compare yourself to may have
many problems you can't see.
There is an easy cure...STOP IT!

Marissa: The only things you should compare yourself to are your goals and your dreams. When you shoot for the moon and miss you will always land among the stars.

Jenna: In today's world it is easy to compare yourself to those who appear to be the best. Remember they are just like you and may have more problems than you think.

Annie: Comparison can feel good if we feel like we are somehow better than someone else. Comparison can make us feel pretty bad when we feel we are less than someone else. The best way to avoid these situations is to be happy with and accept yourself.

Your Thoughts

"I Don't Know"

Unknown

These three words can be liberating.
You don't need to lie or make up a story.
You don't need to remember what you said before.
It is far better to say "I don't know" than to get into
a situation you may later regret.
IT IS OK TO NOT KNOW SOMETHING.

Annie: No one is all knowing. Don't be afraid to let someone know you don't know. Try to find the right answer to the question to gain more knowledge.

Jenna: Sometimes it may be hard to hurt your pride by admitting you don't know something. You may hurt yourself even more by trying to make something up.

Marissa: "I don't know" will always set you free.

Your Thoughts

You Will Learn Lessons.
There Are No Mistakes-Only Lessons.
A Lesson Is Repeated Until
It Is Learned.
If You Don't Learn Easy Lessons,
They Get Harder.
(Pain Is One Way To Get Your Attention)
You Know You've Learned A Lesson When
Your Actions Change.

Unknown

People become reluctant to change as they age.
It takes more to get their attention.
However, they also have the wisdom already gained
from lessons learned.

Marissa: When your heart aches to take something back, you have learned a great lesson. Welcome to the rest of your life.

Jenna: Never fear change, embrace the lessons and make the most of them. Most importantly, we have to recognize the lessons in our failures.

Annie: We all make mistakes—the sooner we learn a lesson from the mistakes the sooner we can move on to our next mistake and our next learning experience.

Your Thoughts

They Call Her Aunt Only When The Cucumbers Are Ripe

Burmese Proverb

People are usually nicer when they want something
you can give them.
As soon as they get what they want they
disappear again.

*Marissa: My nephews and nieces always
call me Marissa unless they really want
me to do something for them. All of a
sudden their voices get sweet and I am
"Aunt Marissa".*

*Jenna: It is important to know your true
friends, because many people will use you
to get what they need. It happens a lot in
high school. Think of when someone
forgot to do their homework and they
treat you super nice and then ask to
borrow your homework.*

*Annie: Some people do things with a
motive behind them to achieve or obtain
what they want.*

Your Thoughts

Have Patience With All Things, But First Of All With Yourself

St. Francis of Sales

We are often much harder on ourselves than
anyone else would ever be.
You WILL make mistakes, because you are human.
If you learn something, are they really mistakes?
If you have hurt someone make amends then let go.

Marissa: This is something I really need to work on. It is very hard to accept there are some things we are unable to do. Be careful to know your limits and accept the things you cannot change.

Jenna: When you are trying something new, you must practice patience. You are bound to screw up a few times but by waiting and working you can do great things. Never get frustrated because it gets in the way of improvement.

Annie: Patience with yourself is needed for you to learn, love, and grow as an individual. It doesn't come easy, but once you develop it within yourself it will be easier to have patience with others.

Your Thoughts

Help Your Brother's Boat Across, And Your Own Will Reach The Shore

Hindu Proverb

When you help others without any thought of reward, this kindness will likely come back to you. Maybe it is GOD's way of saying thanks.

Jenna: You shouldn't do something for the reward, but for the good feeling you get when helping others.

Annie: Kind acts will come back to you 10-fold one day.

Marissa: When you guide someone towards their goal, you might find yourself a bit closer to your own.

Your Thoughts

In Reading The Lives Of Great Men, I Found That The First Victory They Won Was Over Themselves...Self-Discipline With All Of Them Came First

Harry S. Truman

If you don't have control over your own thoughts
and behaviors, how do you expect to
achieve anything?
Everything begins with self-discipline.
The word "self" is in there for a reason.

Jenna: You can't blame others for your mistakes. Instead, go back and find where you screwed up and fix it yourself.

Marissa: You really can't love, trust, or like someone else until you do so with yourself.

Annie: In the process of learning self-discipline we have the opportunity to learn who we are on the inside. It's not until we know who we are and what our goals are that we are able to accomplish things which make us "great".

Your Thoughts

Character Is Like A Tree And Reputation Like Its Shadow. The Shadow Is What We Think Of It; The Tree Is The Real Thing

Abraham Lincoln

Shadows come and go.
Reputations can change nearly as often.
The tree, like your character, has roots and doesn't get to change as easily.
Your character can only be changed with much effort and hard work.

Annie: Remember that your reputation is at stake in all you do. Even though the tree is the real you—people tend to see the shadow. Your actions speak volumes about your character.

Marissa: Your character will always have a shadow. Similar to that of a tree, it will grow and change. Make sure your character is strong and steady so that the shadow reflects a wonderful person.

Jenna: Be true to who you are and not what people WANT you to be. If you slip up it will soon be forgotten.

Your Thoughts

25

The Angry Man Will Defeat Himself In Battle As Well As Life

Samurai Maxim

When angry no one thinks clearly or makes
good decisions.
Being angry can lead to behavior you end up feeling
guilty about later.

Annie: Anger is a losing battle.

Marissa: Anger leads to doing and saying things we might regret in the future. If you feel yourself getting revved up inside, take some deep breaths. If that doesn't help, walk away until you can face the situation with a clear mind.

Jenna: How many times have you fought with your parents and said hurtful words you didn't mean? It is always best to talk after you have all cooled down.

Your Thoughts

26

Worry Often Gives A Small Thing A Big Shadow

Swedish Proverb

Instead of confronting some problem immediately,
you neglect it, hoping it will go away.
The problem doesn't go away and you begin using
energy worrying about it.
The vast majority of what you worry about cannot
be changed.
It may be necessary to seek counseling if worry is
beginning to dominate your life.
THOUGHTS CAN BE CHANGED.

Annie: Fears and anxiety can make problems appear bigger than they really are.

Jenna: How many times have you worried over a test and made it harder than it actually was?

Marissa: Stop worrying about things you cannot control. You get so worked up you will forget to live.

Your Thoughts

27

The "C" Students Run The World

Harry S. Truman

Grades are only a measure of one specific subject.
Grades determine absolutely nothing
in how well you will do in life.
Determination is much more important.

Marissa: Both Julia Roberts and Jay Leno were "C" students. You don't have to be a brilliant "A+" rocket scientist to make something of yourself.

Jenna: High school is not always about grades. Many students try very hard and can only get a "C" while some may not have to try and they always get the "A". Even though they have the "A", they don't always have the willingness to work and succeed that the "C" student has.

Annie: The leaders of the world do not strive for perfection but attempt to find a balance.

Your Thoughts

28

You Must Live Your Life From Beginning To End; No One Else Can Do It For You

Hopi Indian Saying

It is up to you what you get out of life.
You will likely have periods of hardship and
disappointment somewhere along the way.
How you REACT to these challenges may
determine whether or not you find happiness.

Jenna: Live life to the fullest and don't be afraid to try new things. You never know what you are missing.

Marissa: Take one step at a time and love every minute of it. Don't go to places you don't want to be and make your choices wisely. Do things the way YOU want them done.

*Annie: Don't depend on others to make your life what you want it to be.
Set yourself goals and strive to reach them so you can one day look back and be proud and satisfied for leading the life you wanted.*

Your Thoughts

29

GOD Grant Me The Serenity To Accept The Things I Cannot Change, Courage To Change The Things I Can, And The Wisdom To Know The Difference

Reinhold Niebuhr

Some things in life you will never be able to change
no matter how hard you try.
Many problems such as alcoholism in your family
you will be powerless to change.
YOU CAN'T CHANGE ANYONE ELSE.
The only person you can change in this
whole world is
YOU.

*Annie: Some things in life are beyond our
control. Focus your attention on the
things which we are able to control.
Use care in determining what things we
do or do not have control of.*

*Marissa: Sometimes it is very hard to tell
the difference between these two things.
Explore yourself. Discover your strengths
and limits, and then you can live
by this prayer.*

*Jenna: Being able to change yourself is
one of our greatest gifts.*

Your Thoughts

30

Conflict Is Inevitable

Unknown

Within any group or team there will be conflicts
between individuals and with the leader.
Why try to stop it?
You may only deprive the group of a possible
learning experience as they struggle to
find a solution.
Accept that conflict will happen and learn better
ways to overcome it. Some leaders try to change
the mood of the group and make everyone happy.
It simply doesn't work. Often a better solution
comes about because of the conflict.

*Jenna: When conflict arises whether it be
with parents or friends, it is always better
to work things out. You may have to wait
and cool down, but embrace the conflict
and always view both sides of the issue.
Both sides may have good ideas.*

*Marissa: You can't change anyone.
You can only change yourself.*

*Annie: Conflict is necessary for growth
and learning.*

Your Thoughts

31

No Man Has A Good Enough Memory To Be A Successful Liar

Abraham Lincoln

Lying takes a keen memory of what you have told others before. The greater the lie, the more you have to remember. The more people lied to, the greater the fear of discovery. Not many lies are worth that much effort.

Marissa: Lying is like smoking, it's addictive. If you don't start, you will never have to quit.

Annie: "Oh, what a web we weave when we practice to deceive".   Unknown.

Jenna: Lies need to be constantly built upon. You tell one small lie, but then you have to lie to make the first lie make sense.   The constant buildup of lies will never get better. The truth in the end is ALWAYS easier.

Your Thoughts

32

He Who Is Present At A Wrongdoing And Does Not Lift A Hand To Prevent It Is As Guilty As The Wrongdoers

Omaha Indian Saying

There is a point where you can no longer turn your head and pretend something isn't happening. There will be times when you MUST take action. What if something was happening to you and nobody did anything to help?

Marissa: Have you ever heard the term "guilt by association"? You too, can be considered guilty for someone else's bad actions.

Jenna: Although it may not be your nature to help the "geeky" kid, they need a friend just like you. Don't let others keep hurting someone, especially if they are judging them instead of getting to know them.

Annie: Being present and NOT stopping a wrong or bad situation, makes you involved. Stand up for what you believe in. If you see something bad being done, SPEAK UP!

Your Thoughts

33

When One Door Of Happiness Closes, Another One Opens. But Often We Look So Long At The Closed Door That We Do Not See The One That Has Been Opened For Us

Helen Keller

Do you keep hoping some situation will magically
turn out the way we want it to?
Maybe it is a relationship which ended and we
keep hoping it would be like it was before.
It may be time to see the door is closed and
move on.

*Annie: Don't get caught up in your
failures, learn from them and move on.*

*Jenna: It is important in life to let things
go and move on because we never know
what good might be right around the
corner.*

*Marissa: As teenagers we worry about so
many trivial things that seem to be a
huge deal at the time. We need to take a
step back from ourselves and view the
situation as an outsider.*

Your Thoughts

34

He Who Leaves His House In Search Of Happiness Pursues A Shadow

Unknown

Your happiness begins and ends with you.
Whether you see happiness or sorrow is in how you
CHOOSE to see any situation.
Trying to find happiness in possessions or through
other people may only cause you misery.

Annie: People often say "the grass is greener on the other side". When you leave in search of something more you may find it is not always better.

Marissa: Happiness is only found within yourself.

Jenna: You have to make your own happiness by working hard and striving for your potential. If you don't try your hardest all the time you will be let down.

Your Thoughts

35

The Person Who Doesn't Read Has No Advantage Over The Person Who Doesn't Know

Unknown

Make time every day to read something.
A newspaper, book, magazine or comic book,
it doesn't matter.
The more you read the more you will gain knowledge.

Annie: To have the ability to read gives you no advantage over the illiterate if you choose not to take the time to expand your mind.

Marissa: Reading is like riding a bike; you slowly get better and better at it. You will learn something from every little thing you read. Intelligence is not something you can buy or receive; it is something you work towards.

Jenna: Reading can strengthen your knowledge and open your mind. It is not just about facts, but also imagination and dreams. Never be afraid to learn.

Your Thoughts

36

Do Not Spit Into The Well—
You May Have To Drink Out Of It

Russian Proverb

What actions you do today you might end up
regretting tomorrow.
The results of your thoughtless actions may return
to cause you big problems.

*Annie: "Don't burn any bridges".
They might eventually be your only escape
from the island later.*

*Jenna: Many times I have said something
about someone close to me in the heat of
things and not meant it. Sooner or later
it always gets back to me.*

*Marissa: It may seem like a cool thing to
do when all of your friends are starting
rumors about people or destroying their
things. What is the purpose of acting that
way? One thing I always try to live by is
to live as though your actions will ALWAYS
come back to you.*

Your Thoughts

37

You Gain Strength, Courage, And Confidence By Each Experience In Which You Really Stop To Look Fear In The Face. You Are Able To Say To Yourself, "I Have Lived Through This Horror. I Can Take The Next Thing That Comes Along"

Eleanor Roosevelt

You are much stronger than you realize.

Jenna: It is the hardest things in life we learn the most from.

Marissa: Sometimes we have time to prepare for being scared. At other times fear just blindsides us.

Annie: With each hardship you have you gain the ability to know you can make it through anything put in your way.

Your Thoughts

38

Life Is Unfair

John F. Kennedy

Whoever told you life would be fair?
Some people feel everyone else has it better than
they do. You can't judge unless you could be the
other person for a while and that is impossible.
Acceptance that life can be unfair will help you
more than complaining about your problems.

*Annie: Not everything happens the way
we would like it to. Accept this and
move on.*

*Marissa: Life IS unfair! Accept this truth
and learn to love your life as it is.*

*Jenna: How many times have you heard
someone say "Life isn't fair"? As much as
we don't want to admit it, it is true. By
accepting this you will be happier because
you will no longer compare what you
have to everyone else.*

Your Thoughts

39

Don't Try To Protect Others From Themselves

Unknown

You will only lose in the long run.
You may become involved in THEIR problem,
which could cause you personal difficulty.
You could help them find information, get help or
just listen. You may deprive them of a learning
situation by getting too involved.

Marissa: Give others the freedom and space to discover themselves. They may not like the person they are becoming but that is not your problem. The only person you can fix is yourself.

Jenna: There is nothing wrong with supporting a friend, but they need to learn from their situations too. Don't take the blame if you didn't do something to help them and don't try to force your ideas on them.

Annie: We can be our own worst enemy. To let someone discover this on their own and make the necessary changes will teach them more than you trying to save them.

Your Thoughts

40

If You Worry What Others Think Of You, You Become Their Prisoner

Unknown

THE ONLY POWER PEOPLE HAVE OVER YOU
IS THE POWER YOU GIVE THEM.
It is ONLY opinions they express.
You become their prisoner by buying into
what "they" think.
YOU control the power over "their" opinions.

Annie: If you become consumed by wondering what others think of you, you have given them the lock and key to your emotions.

Marissa: If you allow other people to dictate the things you do and the way you act you aren't being yourself. You need to be happy with yourself before you can be completely happy with anything else.

Jenna: In high school kids feel a need to follow the popular crowd, but when you try to do this too hard you become who THEY want you to be instead of being yourself.

Your Thoughts

41

GOD Gave Us Two Ears And One Mouth To Be Used In That Proportion

Irish Proverb

Try to listen twice as much as you speak.
Resist the temptation to speak BEFORE you think.
Learn to concentrate on what others are saying and
NOT just thinking of what you plan to say.

Jenna: In high school you can learn a lot from listening to others, not just teachers. When you listen carefully you can distinguish fact from fiction and avoid spreading rumors.

Annie: Learn to give others the focus and attention you want when they are speaking.

Marissa: Learn from the mistakes other people make. Hear what they have to say and see how other people react to your comments.

Your Thoughts

42

Never Answer A Letter While You Are Angry

Chinese Proverb

Resist the urge to email or call back immediately.
No good will come of it.
If you must reply, write a letter and stick it in a
safe place until you have cooled down.
You will likely be glad you didn't mail the letter or
send the email.

*Annie: A letter written in anger may
have words in it which are best unsaid
until you reevaluate whether or not it is
what you really mean.*

*Marissa: Most angry words will cause
more hurt than intended. Words on
paper can be especially painful. The
receiver has the ability to read these
hurtful words over and over again
causing even more hurt and anger
than before.*

*Jenna: When angry we often say things
without thinking. So cool down and then
reply. Be especially careful with e-mails
and instant messages because people are
even more likely to answer hurriedly and
with anger.*

Your Thoughts

43

Great Minds Discuss Ideas. Average Minds Discuss Events. Small Minds Discuss People.

Eleanor Roosevelt

How often do you talk about other people?
How much of it is gossip?

Jenna: Everyone knows how it feels to be talked about, so why do we continue to talk about others?

Marissa: Don't be afraid to ask questions when it comes to learning more about important and crucial information. The more you know the less likely you are to discuss rumors.

Annie: It takes a lot more thought and effort to discuss complex things like ideas—anyone can talk about someone else.
Do you choose to stand out?

Your Thoughts

44

If The Blind Lead The Blind, Both Shall Fall Into The Ditch

Matthew 15:14

Be careful of who you follow.
Anyone who blindly follows another without using his/her judgment may pay a heavy price if that person is wrong.

Jenna: Just because someone is popular doesn't mean their ideas are the best. Ask questions and pursue what you want to do.

Annie: If you know someone is wrong do not blindly or willingly follow them down the wrong path.

Marissa: Don't let anyone lead you. Walk side by side and take the journey together.

Your Thoughts

45

Clear Your Mind Of "Can't"

Solon

"Can't" is one word we use which keeps us stuck.
This word can creep in and keep us from even
making an attempt to try something new.
Saying "I can't" means the same thing as "I won't".

Marissa: I like to tell my students that "can't" is not a word I allow in my classroom. I don't believe in the word. If you don't know how to do something, don't be afraid to say so. Saying "can't" lowers your self-esteem.

Annie: "Can't" lets fear grow in us and it stops us from trying. Believe in yourself, you can do anything you put your mind to.

Jenna: Saying "I can't" may be an excuse to not attempt something new. People often use "can't" when they aren't good at something to get out of it. If you continue to say "can't" you will never be able to succeed because you won't try new experiences.

Your Thoughts

46

Many Things Are Lost For Want Of Asking

English Proverb

Have you ever been afraid to ask for help?
How do you know what someone else is going to say
before you ask?
What is the absolute worst that could happen?
They say "no".
Why are you still reluctant to ask?
There are times when you NEED to ask for help.
You do have enough courage to ask for help.

*Marissa: Don't live your life in fear.
Ask questions. Ask lots of questions. If one
person doesn't know the answer,
ask someone else.*

Annie: If you don't ask, you can't receive.

*Jenna: Never be afraid to ask for help.
If you don't understand something ASK!
By asking you are bettering yourself
because another's ideas could
be very helpful.*

Your Thoughts

47

If You Always Live With Those Who Are Lame, You Will Yourself Learn To Limp

Latin Proverb

You will begin to act like the people you hang around with.
If you are not comfortable with their actions or attitudes find different friends.
You will be judged by the company you keep.

Annie: Beware of others' influence on you—our friends rub off on us. Be sure to choose your friends carefully.

Marissa: Surround yourself with happy and positive people and you will be a happy and positive person.

Jenna: People you hang out with tend to rub off on you. Everyone judges you by who your friends are, so be careful who you choose.

Your Thoughts

48

Not Everyone Patting You On Your Back Is Your Friend And Not Everyone Yelling At You is Your Enemy

Unknown

Anytime people throw lots of praise on
you...BEWARE.
The one praising may have other motives.
Sometimes, friends may yell at you because they
have an important point to get across.

Jenna: I once had a coach who did not believe in lots of praise, but constructive criticism. It was hard to get used to, but I improved because I was being told what I was doing wrong.

Annie: Ever heard the saying... "keep your friends close and your enemies closer"? Sometimes people who you think are close friends have other intentions and can hurt you the most.

Marissa: Praise seems so wonderful and you may have special feelings for those who give you praise. The thing you need to look for is the reasoning behind the praise. The people who love and care for you not only give you praise but will also give you constructive criticism.

Your Thoughts

49

Silence Is Sometimes The Answer

Estonian Proverb

When you aren't sure what to say don't say
anything.
For some things there are simply no answers.
Sometimes just being there for someone will be all
that you can do.

Annie: Silence allows time for reflection and time to gather your thoughts.

Jenna: This reminds me of the common quote most have heard when they were little, "If you have nothing nice to say, don't say anything at all".

Marissa: Some of the best conversations I have had with friends and family have contained no words.

Your Thoughts

50

Nearly All Men Can Stand Adversity, But If You Want To Test A Man's Character, Give Him Power

Abraham Lincoln

Many people (including teens) when given a position of power will become corrupt and abuse their power.
The person you knew and the person recently given power may act like two separate people.

Jenna: I have seen this happen on a soccer team. A girl named captain suddenly became bossy and demanding especially in the coach's presence. It is good to lead, but don't abuse your power.

Marissa: People act differently among different crowds. When a leader abuses the power they are given, you will know what kind of person they really are.

Annie: When everyone is on our side and we have the power to influence, we often fail because the power is so mighty that we forget who we really are.

Your Thoughts

51

Sometimes It Rains On The Just. I Believe That. Sometimes It Rains On The Unjust. I Believe That Too. But I Also Believe That Sometimes It Just Rains. Neither GOD Or Justice Has Anything To Do With It.

Anon.

Sometimes things just happen.
There is no logical reason why they happen and all
the thinking in the world won't come up
with a reason.
Much of what happens in life you must learn to
accept and be able to make the best of what
you have.

Jenna: Don't spend time trying to figure out why something happened. It is best to accept it and move on because many times there are no real answers.

Marissa: Sometimes you just have to learn to deal with it.

Annie: It's just like in the cards—anyone can get dealt the bad hand—just by chance.

Your Thoughts

52

I Don't Need A Friend Who Changes When I Change And Who Nods When I Nod; My Shadow Does That Much Better

Plutarch

A true friend will be able to challenge your beliefs. You don't need friends who follow you blindly and you certainly don't need to copy someone else.

Marissa: If you don't act like yourself then who are you acting like? It is a lot easier to be yourself than to try to impress people by being something you are not. If they don't like you for who you are, it is their loss and you don't need them as friends.

Annie: Friends don't say and do things to impress you or to be "popular". Friends say and do things because they are your friend and are looking out for you.

Jenna: Have you ever noticed the clique in school that is led by one "popular" girl who has many "followers"? These girls do everything the leader does and they rarely show their own personality. Be unique and true to yourself.

Your Thoughts

53

Yard By Yard, It's Very Hard. But Inch By Inch, It's A Cinch

Anon.

Say you have some huge project due for class or your
job. Even thinking about it seems overwhelming.
You begin to convince yourself you'll never finish.
Set a small goal like the title page.
Finish that.
Not so hard was it?
Then set another goal.
By focusing on just a part of the problem it won't
seem so huge.

*Annie: Baby steps will get you to the
finish line.*

*Jenna: You need to start small. If you
jump into something it's only going to be
harder in the long run.*

*Marissa: Take It Slow! If you speed
through relationships, homework, chores,
or life you are missing the enjoyment of it
all. Find something new and interesting
about your homework. At the end of every
day, reflect and be proud of what you
have done.*

Your Thoughts

54

Look For The Good In Everything

Unknown

Things happen in your life which you consider
terrible at the time. After more time and thought
you may find some benefit actually came from
what happened.
Try to see the good things that happen.

*Marissa: Everything happens for a reason
and there will always be a bright side.
My brother died at a young age but at
least I had a very special friend for
ten years. Time heals all wounds and the
sun will shine again.*

*Annie: Everything and everyone has good
in it. Sometimes we just have to look
deeper for it.*

*Jenna: I think this saying applies best to
enemies. Even if you don't like someone
that doesn't mean they are all bad.*

Your Thoughts

55

The Greatest Griefs Are Those We Cause Ourselves

Sophocles

Our own thoughts cause many of our problems.
They are only thoughts and nothing more.
Thoughts have NO power except what we
GIVE them.
THOUGHTS CAN ALWAYS BE CHANGED.

Jenna: Many times I find myself over-thinking and over-analyzing everything. When I realize this I stop and go back to the beginning. I usually find an easy solution or no problem at all.

Annie: Some of the things we feel most sad and guilty about are situations we cause by our thoughts, words, or actions. Keep this in mind to put any situation in perspective.

Marissa: Many times we get angry at ourselves because of the way we handled a situation. Thinking before speaking or acting will help diminish some of the grief and anger.

Your Thoughts

56

Be Kind, For Everyone You Meet Is Fighting A Hard Battle

Plato

Those you meet may be struggling with the weight
of many problems just like you.
Why not provide some simple kindness like a smile
or a homemade card?
You are never alone in any battle.

Marissa: Be supportive of people and their
decisions. You may not approve of the
things they are doing and that is OK.
But remember you don't know the entire
story behind someone else's actions.
You never know when you may be the one
needing support.

Annie: Many days your problems may be
so overwhelming you feel like you are
fighting the hardest battle of your life.
Stop and remember that many people
have it far worse than you. Be kind to
everyone, you never know who has a
bigger problem than you on that day.

Jenna: Never think you are the only
person with problems. In high school
don't use problems as an excuse to be
mean and angry. Be thankful to be alive
and greet everyone with a smile.

Your Thoughts

57

What You Have Said In The Dark Will Be Heard In The Daylight, And What You Have Whispered In The Ear In The Inner Rooms Will Be Proclaimed From The Roofs

Luke 12:3

What you think is hidden away will come out.
What you think nobody knows will
eventually spread.
What you say will eventually be heard by everyone.

Jenna: This is very true. Words travel very quickly, especially in a small school like mine. You need to be careful what you say.

Annie: Be careful what you say in confidence to someone—secrets get out.

Marissa: Even if you think you are doing something in secret, someone may see. Figure out the difference between the people you can and cannot trust. Words can spread like a wild fire.

Your Thoughts

58

The Teacher Opens The Door But The Student Must Walk Through

Taoist Proverb

We are all students.
We are all teachers.
A teacher can't force you to learn.
The choice of what you learn is up to you.
You are the one who has to do the work and WANT
to learn.

Jenna: We have to be open to what others say, no matter who they are. You can learn something from everyone.

Annie: Opportunities to learn will be provided by others, but we need to WANT to learn to gain anything.

Marissa: One of my students started calling me "K.P." I brought it to his attention that it was disrespectful and they weren't even my initials. He smiled, apologized and said "But I believe in you and you believe in me and that is K.P. His definition of K.P. was "Knowledge is Power".

Your Thoughts

59

Habits Are First Cobwebs, Then Cables

Spanish Proverb

When bad habits are first practiced they are
easy to break.
The longer habits are practiced the more difficult
they are to change.
This is why it is so important to have good teachers
or role models when first learning something new.

*Annie: Habits start small, but with time
and practice they start to become
all consuming.*

*Jenna: Bad habits are the hardest to
break. Take them slowly with
perseverance and you will get there.
One bad habit you should never start
is smoking. It becomes a "cable" way
too fast.*

*Marissa: When you try to break an old
habit, you have to learn how to live
differently. Some habits when trying to
quit like smoking or drinking forces you
to change your life style. If you quit the
habit as it begins, you will not have so
many drastic changes.*

Your Thoughts

60

Don't Walk Behind Me; I May Not Lead
Don't Walk In Front Of Me; I May Not Follow.
Walk Beside Me That We May Be As One

Ute Indian Saying

No one is better than you.
You are no better than anyone else.

Annie: What do you look for in a friend?
Do you look for someone who will do
things just because you do them? Do you
look for someone to tell you what to do?
Or do you look for someone who will let
you be you and help you along the way?

Jenna: Although you may not think so,
you are equal to everyone. Money and
possessions mean nothing in the long run.

Marissa: When I walk behind, you can't
see me. When you walk behind, I can't see
you. When we walk side by side, we get to
share our journey.

Your Thoughts

61

Anyone Can Be Polite To A King, But It Takes A Civilized Person To Be Polite To A Beggar

Unknown

Are you polite to those who have nothing to offer you?
Do you say please and thank you to those people working behind any counter?

Annie: Since we were young, it has been reinforced in us to be polite to people older and of higher status than us (socially, financially, or academically) because we may someday get something out of the relationship. Always remember the Golden Rule—treat others as you would like to be treated.

Marissa: Living in Chicago for 4 years taught me a lot about life. I learned I should never whine too much because there is always someone who is worse off than I am.

Jenna: Being polite to the king is sometimes like sucking-up to the most influential person. It doesn't matter how nice you are to them when you treat others badly.

Your Thoughts

62

It Was Only A Sunny Smile
And Cost Little In Giving.
But Like Morning Light,
It Scattered The Night,
And Made The Day Worth Living

Anon

A simple smile contains so much power.
A simple act such as smiling can change those
around.   You'll often see them smiling back.

*Jenna: Something as simple as a smile
can turn someone's day around. Always
wear a smile because you never know who
you'll meet.*

*Marissa: Never frown; you don't know who
is falling in love with your smile.*

*Annie: One small smile or one kind word
takes such little effort but has the ability
to dissolve all of our bad thoughts and
feelings for the whole day.*

Your Thoughts

63

He Who Does Not Know How To Serve Cannot Know How To Command

Yugoslavian Proverb

If you have never been at the bottom, how can you
know what the bottom is like?
If you haven't felt what it is like to be ordered
around then you can't lead.

Annie: Start at the bottom to get to the top. You need to know the basics of a job to be able to teach it to others.

Jenna: Being a leader is one of the most important qualities a person can possess. In order to fully apply this quality a person must know what it is like at the other end to be able to know how people feel.

Marissa: It is a lot easier to lead when you have been in the position of the people you are leading. We learn best through experience and we can teach others when we know exactly what they are going through.

Your Thoughts

64

Great Things Are Done By A Series Of Small Things Brought Together

Vincent van Gogh

Most people only see the result of an action, not the small steps and actions which accumulated to make the final result.
Everything you do begins with a small step.

Marissa: Look at anything around you; a beautiful yard is made up of millions of simple blades of grass or a painting by van Gogh is made up of small brush strokes to make a priceless painting. Start small.

Annie: Just as many particles make up one element, many small accomplishments or tasks make up one great success.

Jenna: Think of sports, in basketball only the scorer gets the glory, but what about the passer? In baseball, the player who hits the home runs gets the fame, but what about the defense? Don't forget the help people offered you along the way too.

Your Thoughts

65

The Snow Goose Need Not Bathe To Make Itself White. Neither Need You Do Anything But Be Yourself

Unknown

Trying to be something other than what or who you are just doesn't work.
People can always tell when you are trying to be something you are not.

Jenna: Kids always seem to want to follow the "popular" crowd. It is better to be yourself than be someone you're not.

Annie: Be true to yourself—people will respect you more if you let your true colors show.

Marissa: You can't love anyone else until you learn how to love yourself unconditionally. Always be yourself. The world will only love you for who you are, nothing more, nothing less.

Your Thoughts

66

A Mistake Is Not A Failure, But Evidence That Someone Tried To Do Something

Anon.

If you try something new you WILL make mistakes.
Too many teens (and adults) consider mistakes as something to be avoided.
Many people avoid them by not trying anything new until someone else has paved the way.
Success can come from simply trying.

Annie: A mistake should never be seen as a failure, rather an opportunity for growth.

Marissa: You are not a failure and don't let anyone convince you otherwise. Anything you do will be a positive learning experience no matter how it turns out. You will NEVER be a failure if you keep trying.

Jenna: It is difficult growing up in a society that looks highly on perfection and frowns on anything except the best. Even though this is true someone has stepped outside the box to invent all things we have today and they each had their share of mistakes before they had successes. Use your mistakes to your advantage.

Your Thoughts

67

For One Word We Are Often Deemed Wise; For One Word We Are Often Deemed Foolish

Chinese Proverb

Choose your words carefully in every situation.
One word you didn't take time to think about could
cause you endless problems.
Think twice, speak once.

Jenna: Be careful what you say about others, It WILL get back to them and cause hard feelings.

Marissa: Listen to the words in your head BEFORE you say them. Make sure your thoughts are clear and you will not be offending anyone.

Annie: One word can change everything.

Your Thoughts

68

What Breaks In A Moment May Take Years To Mend

Swedish Proverb

Hearts and friendships can quickly be broken by
some comment you didn't take time to think about.
It may seem insignificant to you, but your comment
may crush the person it is aimed at.
Learn to think before you speak.

*Jenna: It is way too easy to lose a friend,
or your parent's trust through careless
action or speech. It often takes a long
time to gain them back.*

*Annie: Thoughtless actions can break a
bond that took years to form. It may take
years to rebuild that bond—if at all.
So always remember... "think twice,
speak once".*

*Marissa: Watch what you say. Even if you
intend for something to be a joke, it could
really hurt someone's feelings. Words can
be the most painful of all evils.*

Your Thoughts

69

We Learn Little From Victory, Much From Defeat

Japanese Proverb

When things are going well, it is unlikely people
will want to make changes.
It is easier to be receptive to new ideas when you
just got your butt kicked.

*Annie: Defeat forces us to look at what we
can change to make improvements.
Victory only looks at the outcome, not the
means it took to get there.*

*Jenna: It is hard to realize what we are
doing wrong when we come out ahead
because you always focus on the positives.
Only when things go really wrong do we
focus on the problems that led to defeat.*

*Marissa: Remember when we got picked
first for the neighborhood team? We were
on top of the world. If we were picked last
we felt defeated. The defeat made us
realize two things: I am better at
something else or I am going to try
harder and one day I will be the one
picking teams.*

Your Thoughts

70

The Race Is Not Always To The Swift, Nor The Battle To The Strong

Ecclesiastes 9:11

Determination alone can help you achieve many things in life. The ability to keep after your dreams regardless of all the problems, setbacks, and people saying you can't do something is a valuable asset.

Jenna: Another huge factor is intelligence. When you use what you already know you can go a long way. Faster is not always better.

Marissa: While being swift and strong can help, persistence should be your guide. NEVER GIVE UP.

Annie: Read the fable of the tortoise and the hare. Speed did not allow the hare to succeed. It was determination and using his head which helped the tortoise overcome his shortcomings.

Your Thoughts

71

It Is Easier To Pull Up An Acorn Than A Mighty Oak Tree

Taoist Wisdom

Learn to see the beginnings of any problem.
It is better to act while a problem is small and
easily fixed than to wait until great effort is needed
to repair it.

*Annie: Changes are easier to make early
on in the game before the stakes get high
and there is a lot more to lose.*

*Marissa: If you are wrong admit it and
when you are right, don't rub it in. When
you love, say so and if you hate, drop it.
Figure out within yourself why things
happen the way they do.*

*Jenna: In high school it is always best to
stop something early, such as slipping
grades. Try to pick them up before they've
hit bottom.*

Your Thoughts

72

Touch Black Paint And You Will Have Black Fingers

Chinese Proverb

Do what your friends want you to do even against your better judgment and you will pay a penalty for not thinking. Make each decision yours without having it based on what someone else wants.

Annie: Common sense is always your best friend. Know what you are getting yourself into.

Marissa: Whether good or bad, your actions will come back to you.

Jenna: All wrong doings have consequences. Even if you don't get caught at first, someone always seems to find out.

Your Thoughts

73

You Do Not Really Know Your Friends From Your Enemies Until The Ice Breaks

Icelandic Proverb

They are all your friends UNTIL some major difficulty hits you. How many "friends" will find reasons to leave when you get into trouble?

Annie: When times are tough, true friends will stay by your side no matter what. The others will find the closest door.

Marissa: The ability to make true friends lies with the type of friend YOU are. When problems affect your friends are you one of the many that run or one of the few which decide to stay?

Jenna: People will always be there when times are good, but when you really need something it is a true friend who supports you and backs you up.

Your Thoughts

74

Never Bend Your Head! Always Hold It High! Look The World Straight In The Face

Helen Keller

Don't shuffle along!
Don't walk with your eyes down and your
shoulders slumped.
Holding your head up automatically improves your
mood and your looks.
Try it.

Annie: Don't be ashamed of who or what you are. Walk proud—the world will see your confidence.

Marissa: In high school my teachers always yelled at me for walking with my head down and my hands in my pockets. I really had to work at good posture and doing something with my hands. Even now, years later, I still fall back into bad habits. What I realized when I looked up was when you are smiling the whole world smiles at you.

Jenna: It is important to hold your head high and have pride in yourself.

Your Thoughts

75

Two People Looked Through Prison Bars, One Saw Mud, The Other Saw Stars

Unknown

If you are in a bad situation which is impossible to change, you can CHOOSE to either see good or bad. If you adjust your thinking and look for the good situations are easier to endure.

Marissa: No matter how bad the situation might be, you need to walk with your head held high. Looking at the dark and dirty will only give you a dark and dirty attitude.

Annie: It is all in how you look at things. Have you ever heard people ask "is the glass half full or half empty"?

Jenna: One time when this is especially important is when you lose a loved one. It is important to focus on the good times you shared, and not the loss.

Your Thoughts

76

If You Do What You've Always Done, You'll Get What You've Always Gotten

Anon.

How easy it is to fall into a rut and just keep doing the same things the exact same way, yet at the same time hoping somehow it will turn out differently. Have the courage to try something different or just do things a different way. Set a goal to attempt something even if it feels scary and you might fail.

Marissa: Try something new every day. It seems crazy but even if it is walking in the left door versus the right door, it will get you to be less repetitive. Change things around, make life interesting.

Annie: We each have a "comfort zone" or a place in life in which we are comfortable and fear very little. This zone can be the best thing or the worst. Go there when comfort is necessary, step out of it for a chance to learn new things and experience new opportunities.

Jenna: If you want something to change you have to step up and change it yourself. No one can do that for you.

Your Thoughts

77

You Have Your Way. I Have My Way. As For The Right Way, And Only Way, It Doesn't Exist

Friedrich Wilhelm Nietzsche

You may believe your way is the ONLY way of doing something. It isn't the only way no matter how convinced you are. It is just one of many options available.

Jenna: Just think of a cookie recipe. There are many different ones, but no matter which you use, you get a delicious cookie.

Annie: There are many paths you can take to reach the same destination. Choose the path which is right for you.

Marissa: If we both get the same correct answer every time, it doesn't matter how we go about getting the solution as long as we used our brains.

Your Thoughts

78

The Good Looking Boy May Be Just Good In The Face

Apache Indian Saying

We often consider someone who is good looking to have more top qualities than they really do.

Jenna: This is way too true in our society. We place too high an emphasis on appearance. This is sad because we may dismiss someone without ever seeing who they really are.

Annie: Looks aren't everything. It is what's inside that's important.

Marissa: Some people who are good looking believe they have power because of their looks. I met a guy who was very good looking but once I got to know him, his personality definitely needed some fine tuning.

Your Thoughts

79

Even Though You Have Ten Thousand Fields You Can Only Eat No More Than One Measure Of Rice A Day. Even Though Your Dwelling Contains A Hundred Rooms, You Can Only Use But Eight Foot Of Space A Night

Chinese Proverb

How much becomes too much?
When do you have enough?
The more you have the more you have to worry about. So much time is wasted worrying someone will take what you have. Are you able to share what you have?

Jenna: Possessions mean nothing in the end, although in high school they can mean popularity and power. Those who appear to have the most may be missing the best possession of all....LOVE.

Annie: What benefit is there in having so many things if you don't have enough time to use them?

Marissa: Are you greedy? It is natural to want a bit of everything. Think about what is necessary and be willing to share with everyone.

Your Thoughts

80

The Girl Who Can't Dance Says The Band Can't Play

Yiddish Proverb

How easy it can be to blame those around us for something we can't do well.

Jenna: In life many people will try to blame everything on others. No one wants to look like the "bad guy". It is important we know what we can do and what we can't do and try to improve.

Marissa: We all say things which might make us look better. The best thing you can do is find your own beat and become your own drummer. Be your own person. Dance like no one is watching.

Annie: Some people find it easier to blame others rather than accept our own shortcomings.

Your Thoughts

81

Help Is Only Help When It Is Perceived As Help

Sign on wall in English Classroom

Unwanted help will often be taken poorly.
It is sometimes wiser to remain silent until asked
for help.

Jenna: I always try to help people at least once, but if they are unwilling to listen and accept my help I don't try a second time. You should always listen to others because they may only offer their help once.

Annie: If someone is not seeking help, offering it may be perceived as more a interference than a help.

Marissa: When my dad would give me help and I didn't want it, I thought he was a jerk. When I asked him for help he turned out to be a great teacher.

Your Thoughts

82

Know How To End Things Well

Unknown

This is something many teens and adults neglect to do. They are all fired up at the beginning but lose interest or energy along the way. Make a real effort to start and end projects with equal zest.

Marissa: Learn to end things with maturity. Always remember that nothing and no one is perfect.

Jenna: Life, in this case, can be compared to a basketball game. A team comes out all fired up and is soon beating their opponent. Then they start slacking off and the other team comes back.
It is important to keep the energy you started with.

Annie: If you give 100% to things from beginning to end, whatever the results you gave it your all. If something ends on a positive note, any mistakes at the beginning become unimportant.

Your Thoughts

83

Nobody's Family Can Hang Up A Sign "Nothing The Matter Here"

Chinese Proverb

Every family has its own share of problems.
You might envy another family but they may just
be better actors.

Marissa: Those families you see on TV and movies are professional actors and aren't related. It may look like heaven but it's not real. Don't feel the need to be like them.

Annie: A family is no different than an individual—no one is perfect.

Jenna: Everyone has his/her own problems. Just because someone's family or life appears great, it doesn't mean they aren't hiding something really difficult.

Your Thoughts

84

To Try Is To Risk Failure. But Risk Must Be Taken As The Greatest Hazard In Life Is To Risk Nothing. The Person Who Risks Nothing, Does Nothing, Has Nothing, And Is Nothing

Unknown

You may fail. You may fail repeatedly. The old saying "you'll never know if you can do something until you try" is true. Many people look back and wish they had done more with their lives. Don't be one of them. Learn to take risks and you will have fewer limits in your life.

Jenna: Once I got over my fears I realized I could do more than I ever thought possible.
My advice: try everything at least once, you may surprise yourself.

Annie: To learn and grow you need to take risks despite fears of failure and rejection.

Marissa: You may shoot for the moon and miss but then you'll end up among the stars. Don't be afraid to succeed.

Your Thoughts

85

If You Don't Have A Plan For Yourself, You'll Be Part Of Someone Else's

American Proverb

You don't want to be part of someone else's plan.
You lose control of your life that way.
Sit down and make a plan for your life.
Where do you want to be in some time frame?
What will you need to make your plan come true?

Jenna: Having a goal in life gives you not just something to work for, but motivation and determination to reach your goal.

Annie: You have the opportunity and power to control what you do and who you are in life. Cherish and take advantage of this or someone else will include you in a plan that's not right for you.

Marissa: Don't let anyone decide for you. Go with your gut instinct. Just because someone else is doing something it doesn't always mean it's the right thing for you. Remember: Sometimes the easy way isn't always right and the right way isn't always easy.

Your Thoughts

86

Think Twice, Speak Once

Unknown

A few words spoken quickly and without thought
can destroy a friendship.
Have patience and think BEFORE you speak.
If you're upset, walk away if necessary until you
are able to think clearly again.

*Jenna: A lot of times when I argue,
especially with my parents, I say
something I don't mean out of anger.
Those words still hurt even though I don't
mean them.*

*Annie: Be thorough in your thinking,
because your spoken word can not be
taken back.*

*Marissa: Someone once said something to
me which was terrible and untrue.
The person said it as a joke. You may
think to yourself "I would never say
anything that mean" or "how could
anyone even think that"?
Without carefully choosing your words
you could say something could hurt just
as deeply.*

Your Thoughts

87

When The Rich Man Falls Down It Is An Accident; When A Poor Man Falls Down, He Is Called A Drunk

Unknown

Alcoholism crosses all social barriers.
Alcoholism makes no distinction between power, money or status.
If alcoholism is a problem in your family, there is help available.
Start at the library or school counselor to start getting educated about their problem.
ALCOHOLISM IS AN EQUAL OPPORTUNITY DESTROYER

Marissa: You have to remember that someone else's drinking problem is not your fault. They may blame it on you or something you did. It is NOT your fault.

Jenna: Basically this is saying that everyone is faced with problems and rough times but we overlook the rich because of their status.

Annie: Be careful in assumptions based only on a person's social status.

Your Thoughts

88

The True Measure Of A Man Is How He Acts When No One Is Watching

Unknown

Many people act one way when others are watching and totally the opposite when they think they are alone. What they act like when they are alone is usually who they really are.

Marissa: Pay attention to what you do differently when no one is watching. Is that who you really are?

Jenna: How many people have you known who always try to do the best and be nice to everyone, but behind closed doors they are the worst gossipers and will do anything to get to the top?

Annie: Some people wear masks when dealing with others. It's when the mask is off that you can see what someone is really like.

Your Thoughts

89

Always Assume Your Guest Is Tired, Cold, And Hungry, And Act Accordingly

Navaho Saying

This is a good saying to remember when you have friends over for the night.

Marissa: Treat others how you want to be treated. Take care of those around you.

Jenna: Many friends will come into your house. Just remember how uncomfortable you feel when you go somewhere new or different. Treat them how you would like to be treated.

Annie: Always look out for the wellbeing of others. It should be kept in mind that you may someday be in their position.

Your Thoughts

90

If I Can Stop One Heart From Breaking I Shall Not Live In Vain. If I Can Ease One Life The Aching Or Cool One Pain Or Help One Fainting Robin Into His Nest Again I Shall Not Live In Vain

Emily Dickinson

You and your actions really DO make a difference in the world. Think of it as throwing a rock into a quiet pond. The ripples spread, bounce around, and then eventually come back. Imagine many ripples caused by kind actions all over the pond.

Jenna: Even if you can only help one person with one small thing, you could be making a huge difference to someone.

Marissa: To the world you may be only one person, but to one person, you may be the world.

Annie: Just helping one person in your life can make it worth living.

Your Thoughts

91

State Your Opinion Then Be Silent

Unknown

How many people have you known who just go on and on about something until everyone loses interest? Learn to speak simply and to the point, then be quiet and listen. People will actually think you are smarter the less you say.

Marissa: Learn how to listen to others. If you feel you have something to say, wait your turn and then speak. Once you have gotten your point across, continue listening. No one likes a person who tries to steal the show.

Annie: Once you state your opinion others will know your thoughts. You don't need to defend your opinion with anyone.

Jenna: Everyone has a right to their opinion. You don't need to explain why you think the way you do. Remember, this may be your perspective but not theirs.

Your Thoughts

92

One Day At A Time

Unknown

This motto used by recovering alcoholics can be
used for other parts of your life.
Some problems seem so huge they seem impossible
to fix. Cut them down to manageable portions.
Just say to yourself you only have to make it
through this day or even the next hour.
You can always do that!

*Marissa: Sometimes high school needs to
be looked at from the point of view of one
day at a time. It was this way for me.
Be determined to overcome each obstacle
as it comes along.*

*Annie: When things begin to seem
overwhelming or too good to be true,
learn to take these situations in smaller
doses (moment to moment or day to day).*

*Jenna: When bad things happen you can
only handle them one day at a time.
If you look too far ahead you may forget
the small important steps to take at the
beginning of recovery.*

Your Thoughts

93

Keep Away From People Who Try To Belittle Your Ambitions. Small People Always Do That, But The Really Great Make You Feel That You, Too, Can Become Great

Mark Twain

Whatever you attempt, someone will say you can't succeed. The people who make fun of you have NO power. The only power is what YOU give them. Ignore what they say and do it anyway.

Jenna: Don't let ANYONE shatter your dreams. They are YOUR dreams and no one has a right to take them away.

Annie: Some people feel better when they see others fail. These are the "small" people who lack their own confidence to succeed.

Marissa: Surround yourself with people who want you to succeed. Some will be your best friends and others may seem like they are constantly nagging at you. Sometimes a small bit of nagging is what you need to keep you on the right track.

Your Thoughts

94

Words Are Mere Bubbles Of Water, But Deeds Are Drops Of Gold

Chinese Proverb

Some of your friends may talk about what they
plan to do…"someday".
The problem is "someday" never arrives.
Take the risk and have the courage to attempt the
dream you haven't told anyone about.
Deeds are important!
Get started today!

*Marissa: Do random acts of kindness.
Don't tell anyone what you did.
Just know within yourself that little
blessings for others will always come
back to you.*

*Jenna: You can talk all you want about
something, but it doesn't mean anything
until you actually get out and do it.*

*Annie: Words are a "dime a dozen".
Good deeds are worth much more.*

Your Thoughts

95

The Reputation Of A Thousand Years May Be Determined By The Conduct Of One Hour

Japanese Proverb

How quickly your life can change by one thoughtless action or word. We can cause much pain when we don't think things through beforehand.

Marissa: We have all been affected by rumors. Be careful what you say about other people.

Annie: A lot of hard work can be ruined by a SINGLE thoughtless word or action.

Jenna: It is always best to think BEFORE you act. I found it is very easy to lose peoples' trust, especially your parents. It only takes one small action to lose that trust, but a great deal of time to gain it back.

Your Thoughts

96

There Is No Medicine To Cure Hatred

West African Proverb

Hatred causes minds to close.
Many people only see what supports their point of
view. They don't want to see those they hate in a
favorable light. To do so would require admitting
they made a mistake. Try to keep hatred from
creeping into your mind.

*Annie: Hatred is very consuming.
There is no quick fix to make it go away.
The only cure is an open mind, an open
heart and forgiveness.*

*Marissa: Don't find reasons to hate
someone. The funny thing about these
feelings is they are probably
reflections of you.
It is up to you to decide how to fix them.*

*Jenna: If you feel someone doesn't like
you it is sometimes better to stay away.
Sometimes time and space are the best
answer to hatred.*

Your Thoughts

97

There Are No Dumb Questions

Unknown

The only way to get answers to your questions is by asking. The only power their opinion has is what YOU give it.
There may be others who have the same question but are afraid to ask and will admire you for asking.

Jenna: Never be afraid to speak up, especially to teachers, coaches and more knowledgeable people. They will respect you for taking the time to understand what they are saying.

Annie: Getting to the right question may start with a "dumb" question, but you need to start somewhere.

Marissa: I learned in college the only "dumb" questions are the ones we DON'T ask. I was struggling in one of my classes but was afraid to speak up. Sometimes we just don't get it and have to ask.

Your Thoughts

98

If It's Working, Keep Doing It.
If It's Not Working, Stop Doing It.
If You Don't Know What To Do,
Don't Do Anything

Medical School Advice

Practice keeping things simple.
This is good advice for any situation.
If you don't know what to do, spend some time and
find out.

Annie: Some people say if it's not broken, don't fix it and if you can't fix it without breaking it, find someone who can.

Marissa: If I could change this quote, I would say "If you don't know what to do, start somewhere". Sometimes the beginning or starting point isn't as clear as we would like it to be.

Jenna: Sometimes it is best to do nothing at all, especially when we are not sure of something. If you find something that works, even if it's not exactly what you expected, keep doing it.

Your Thoughts

99

There But For The Grace Of GOD Goes I

Ancient Saying

I believe this small saying holds enormous
power.
That is why I am placing it next to last.
When you look at your enemies or someone
with severe problems what do you see?
Hatred?
Pity?
Maybe GOD put them here so you could
learn from them and them from you.
With a twist of fate or GOD's wishes the
person you despise or pity could have been
you.
If YOU were that person, how would you
want to be treated?

Your Thoughts

100

It Is Said An Eastern Monarch Once Charged His Wise Men To Invent For Him A Sentence, To Be Ever In View And Appropriate In All Times And Situations. They Presented Him The Words: And This Too, Shall Pass Away

Abraham Lincoln

I will finish with this powerful saying. It can be used in any terrible situation you may find yourself stuck in. If you take anything away from this book, I do hope you will remember this small saying when things are tough.

This Too Shall Pass

Tim A. Gaertner is a graduate of Central Michigan University and is the author of Abc's FOR TEENS GROWING UP WITH AN ALCOHOLIC. He lives in Michigan.

Annie Grauf currently resides in Saginaw, Michigan.. She received her Bachelor's in Social Work from Saginaw Valley State University and moved on to Michigan State University to receive her Master's Degree in Clinical Social Work. Annie currently provides counseling for sexually assaulted children and adults through a non-profit agency in Saginaw.

Marissa Kae Markey graduated from Loyola University in Chicago and is a kindergarten teacher who loves hugs, listening and welcoming new people into her life. She currently resides in Saginaw, Michigan.

Jenna Urban grew up in Saginaw, Michigan and is a 2007 graduate of Nouvel Catholic Central High School. She is a well-rounded student-athlete who participated in basketball, volleyball, and soccer. She is continuing her education at the Central Michigan University and studying graphic design.